Winning 101

Wisdom and Inspiration for
Successful People

Avant-garde Books, LLC

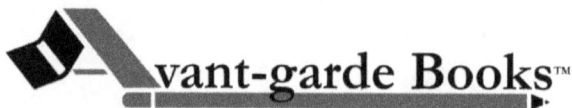

Avant-garde Books™

Avant-garde Books, LLC
Post Office Box 566
Mableton, Georgia 30126
www.avantgardebooks.net

Winning 101:
Wisdom and Inspiration for Successful People

Cover Graphics: Suzanne Horwitz

ISBN: 978-1-946753-44-1

For bulk purchases and discounts for nonprofit organizations, contact Avant-garde Books at avantgardebooks@gmail.com.

Connect with Avant-garde Books, LLC!

f @avantgardebooks100

@Avant_GardeBks

@avantgardebooks

In loving memory of
Cindy Jane Green
(1968-2019),
Daughter, Niece, Sister,
Cousin, Aunt,
Wife, Mother, Educator,
and Philanthropist

Table of Contents

Table of Contents

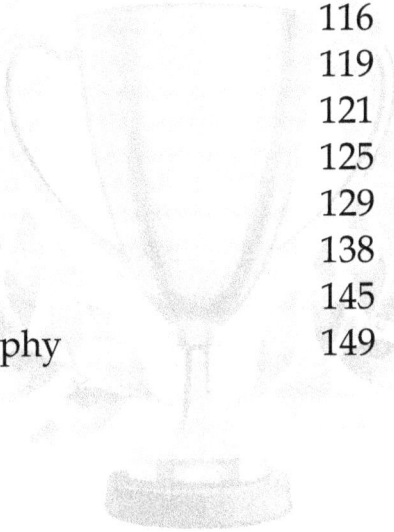

Publisher's Note

"I have learned that success is to be measured not so much by the position that one has reached in life as by the obstacles which he has overcome while trying to succeed."
— Booker T. Washington (1856-1915)

Dear Reader,

In addition to compiling quotes for *Winning 101: Wisdom and Inspiration for Successful People*, I asked several family members and friends to share their definition of success. Interestingly, the responses were as varied as the kinds of flowers in a typical botanical garden. However, the majority I queried, mentioned one common denominator for measuring success: "progress". Most people cited that how far you have come has more significance than where you are now.

As you are reading and reflecting on the transformative and empowering messages in this book, keep in mind that success is not the same for everyone, and it is not a destination; it is a continual journey that integrates a myriad of experiences. There will be days that you enjoy and celebrate the scenic route to your goals. On the other hand, you will also endure long delays, roadblocks, and navigate through detours.

Furthermore, do not accept the delusion that successful people lead perfect lives. No one can boast of a painless, stress-free highway to achievement. In fact, most influential and powerful people can write volumes on setbacks, including disappointment, loss, and failure.

What distinguishes successful people from those who never accomplished their goals? People who achieve extraordinary feats monitor their attitude and they choose to use failure and negative circumstances as powerful, learning tools and steppingstones instead of paralyzing and debilitating, stumbling blocks. Moreover, true winners understand that in order to experience victorious lives and become examples of excellence in their perspective fields of expertise, they must move forward despite their fear of failure. Consider the wisdom of Super Bowl-winning, former NFL coach Tony Dungy: "Don't fear failure; fear being successful at things that don't matter."

To become the endearing hero of your own success story, you do not have to be perfect, but you must employ the life lessons gained from all experiences, whether they are good or bad. This is critical to elevating your mind; progressing as a human being; and potentially empowering yourself and others.

The timeless wisdom that is shared by the people in this book comes from both their hardships as well as their achievements. Influential leaders such as Steve Jobs, Margaret Thatcher, Bill Gates, Tyler Perry, Benjamin Franklin, Oprah Winfrey, Mahatma Gandhi, and Dr. Martin Luther King, Jr. experienced great heartbreak and difficulty during their lives, but they intentionally sought out ways to transform their obstacles into opportunities for greater good, productivity, and creativity.

As successful businessman Jim Rohn (1930-2009) once said, "Successful people do what unsuccessful people are unwilling to do. Never wish life was easier; wish that you were better." Your attitude, character, and integrity will ultimately determine the outcome of your efforts to succeed. Regardless of how tough things might appear, do not give up, especially if you have an unwavering conviction in your heart that you are fulfilling your life's purpose.

My hope is that *Winning 101: Wisdom and Inspiration for Successful People* will help you accomplish noble goals, not just for yourself, but for the betterment of humanity. Stay encouraged no matter how arduous the tasks that you must complete to realize your dreams.

Hold your head up; smile; and never forget that there are always treasures hidden beneath your trouble. Your beating heart is evidence that there is still work for you to do, so keep striving to fulfill your destiny. Look deep within yourself, and you will discover the answers that lead to the precious gems of wisdom, peace, happiness, love, and **SUCCESS**.

Sincerely,
C. Chérie Hardy
Avant-garde Books, LLC

Action

"The only place where success comes before work is in the dictionary."
—Vidal Sassoon

Action

"The way to get started is to quit talking and begin doing." — Walt Disney

"Opportunities are usually disguised as hard work, so most people don't recognize them." — Ann Landers

"You know you are on the road to success if you would do your job, and not be paid for it." — Oprah Winfrey

"I never dreamed about success, I worked for it." — Estée Lauder

"The price of success is hard work, dedication to the job at hand, and the determination that whether we win or lose, we have applied the best of ourselves to the task at hand."
— Vince Lombardi

Action

"Action is the foundational key to all success."-Pablo Picasso

"It's not what we do once in a while that shapes our lives, but what we do consistently." -Tony Robbins

"An ounce of action can crush a ton of fear."-Tim Fargo

"You don't win on emotion. You win on execution." -Tony Dungy

"It is the working man who is the happy man. It is the idle man who is the miserable man." — Benjamin Franklin

"Life is not a spectator sport. If you're going to spend your whole life in the grandstand just watching what goes on, in my opinion you're wasting your life." — Jackie Robinson

Action

"Ideas are a dime a dozen. People who
implement them are priceless."
— Mary Kay Ash

"On the soft bed of luxury many
kingdoms have expired."
— Andrew Young

"Do what works. If your actions are not
producing the results you desire, don't be
afraid to implement something new. If
you want different results, you have to
try something different."
— C. Chérie Hardy

"I have always worked on the idea that if
you have something to worry about, you
get up and go fix it. I've never been a
worrier." — Joe Rogers, Sr.

Action

"I had to make my own living and my own opportunity. But I made it! Don't sit down and wait for the opportunities to come. Get up and make them."
—Madame C. J. Walker

"Success seems to be connected with action. Successful people keep moving. They make mistakes, but they don't quit."
—Conrad Hilton

"Some people want it to happen, some wish it would happen, others make it happen." —Michael Jordan

"No one who can rise before dawn three hundred sixty days a year fails to make his family rich." —Malcolm Gladwell

Attitude

"Attitude, to me, is more important than facts…We cannot change the inevitable… I am convinced that life is 10% what happens to me and 90% how I react to it." — Charles Swindoll

Attitude

"Never wish life were easier, wish that you were better." —Jim Rohn

"It is not your aptitude, but your attitude that determines your altitude."
–Zig Ziglar

"He who cannot change the very fabric of his thought will never be able to change reality, and will never, therefore make any progress." —Anwar Sadat

"If you don't like something, change it. If you can't change it, change your attitude." —Maya Angelou

"Seek to understand rather than be understood." —Stephen R. Covey

"No one can make you feel inferior without your consent."
—Eleanor Roosevelt

Attitude

"Don't be in a hurry to condemn because he doesn't do what you do or think as you think or as fast. There was a time when you didn't know what you know today." — Malcolm X

"You can't always control circumstances. However, you can always control your attitude, approach, and response. Your options are to complain or to look ahead and figure out how to make the situation better." — Tony Dungy

"If you think down, you will go down. If you think up, you will go up. You'll always travel in the direction of your thinking." -T.D. Jakes

"The difference between a successful person and others is not a lack of strength, not a lack of knowledge, but rather a lack of will." — Vince Lombardi

Attitude

"The greatest pollution problem we face today is negativity. Eliminate the negative attitude and believe you can do anything." — Mary Kay Ash

"No matter what happens in your life, find the good. Your attitude can be either positive or negative. The choice is up to you." — Catherine Pulsifer

Change

"You're always one decision away from a totally different life." — Unknown

Change

"Never doubt that a small group of thoughtful, committed, citizens can change the world. Indeed, it is the only thing that ever has."–Margaret Mead

"Change is inevitable; you cannot escape it and resisting change might make things worse. Getting wisdom about how to adapt to change is essential for you to experience success. The most resilient people are those who seek out information that will empower them to do better." — C. Chérie Hardy

"Not everything that is faced can be changed. But nothing can be changed until it is faced." — James Baldwin

"I can be changed by what happens to me, but I refuse to be reduced by it." – Maya Angelou

Change

"When obstacles arise, you change your
direction to reach your goal; you do not
change your decision to get there."
-Zig Ziglar

"Change is the law of life. And those who
look only to the past or present are
certain to miss the future."
—John F. Kennedy

"Change is painful. Few people have the
courage to seek out change. Most people
won't change until the pain of where they
are exceeds the pain of change."
—Dave Ramsey

"Change is a process, not an event."
—Dale C. Bronner

"Arrival at a new destination only occurs
from leaving your current location."
—Chris Hogan

Change

"Life is a series of natural and spontaneous changes. Don't resist them - that only creates sorrow. Let reality be reality. Let things flow naturally forward in whatever way they like." — Lao Tzu

"We live in a changing world, but we need to be reminded that the important things have not changed, and the important things will not change if we keep our priorities in proper order."
— S. Truett Cathy

"The unexamined life is not worth living." — Socrates

"Change the way you look at things and the things you look at change."
— Wayne W. Dyer

"Everyone thinks of changing the world, but no one thinks of changing himself."
— Leo Tolstoy

Character

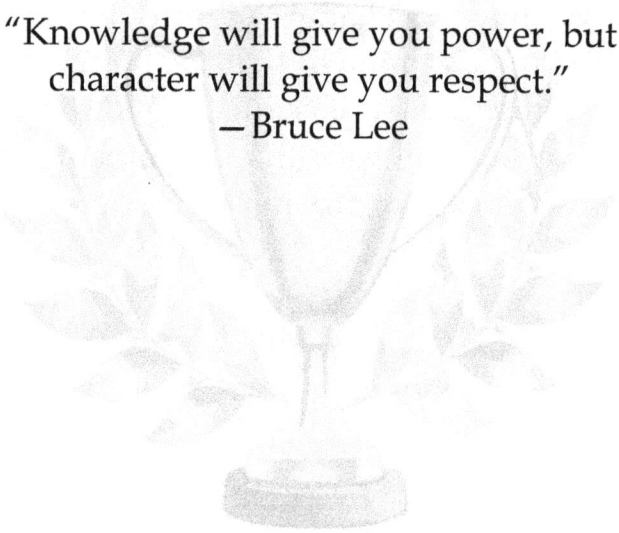

"Knowledge will give you power, but
character will give you respect."
— Bruce Lee

Character

"If you are interested in success, it's easy to set your standards in terms of other people's accomplishments and then let other people measure you by those standards. But the standards you set for yourself are always more important. They should be higher than the standards anyone else would set for you, because in the end you have to live with yourself, and judge yourself, and feel good about yourself. And the best way to do that is to live up to your highest potential. So set your standards high and keep them high, even if you think no one else is looking." — John C. Maxwell

"The ultimate measure of a man is not where he stands in moments of comfort and convenience, but where he stands at times of challenge and controversy."
-Martin Luther King, Jr.

Character

"You can easily judge the character of a man by the way he treats those who can do nothing for him."–James Miles

"Be more concerned with your character than your reputation, because character is what you really are, your reputation is merely what others think you are."
–John Wooden

"Character cannot be developed in ease and quiet. Only through experience through trial and suffering can the soul be strengthened, ambition inspired, and success achieved."–Helen Keller

"Great minds discuss ideas; average minds discuss events; small minds discuss people." —Eleanor Roosevelt

"Try not to become a man of success. Rather become a man of value."
— Albert Einstein

Character

"Character is a quality that embodies many important traits, such as integrity, courage, perseverance, confidence and wisdom. Unlike your fingerprints that you are born with and can't change, character is something that you create within yourself and must take responsibility for changing." — Jim Rohn

"Nearly all men can stand adversity, but if you want to test a man's character, give him power." — Abraham Lincoln

"It takes 20 years to build a reputation and five minutes to ruin it. If you think about that, you'll do things differently." — Warren Buffett

"Real integrity is doing the right thing, knowing that nobody's going to know whether you did it or not." — Oprah Winfrey

Character

"Honesty is the cornerstone of all success, without which confidence and ability to perform shall cease to exist."
— Mary Kay Ash

"The way to gain a good reputation is to endeavor to be what you desire to appear." — Socrates

"You have enemies? Good. That means you've stood up for something, sometime in your life."
— Winston S. Churchill

Community

"A great civilization is not conquered from [the outside] until it has destroyed itself from within." —Will Durant

Community

"The greatness of a community is most accurately measured by the compassionate actions of its members."
— Coretta Scott King

"There is no power for change greater than a community discovering what it cares about." – Margaret J. Wheatley

"In every community, there is work to be done. In every nation, there are wounds to heal. In every heart, there is the power to do it. – Marianne Williamson

"Alone, we can do so little; together, we can do so much" – Helen Keller

"If you want to go quickly, go alone. If you want to go far, go together."
— African Proverb

Community

"As you grow older, you will discover that you have two hands: one for helping yourself and one for helping others."
— Audrey Hepburn

"We should be about more than just selling chicken: we should be a part of our customers' lives and the communities in which we serve." — S. Truett Cathy

"I want you to understand that your first duty is to humanity. I want others to look at us and see that we care not just about ourselves but about others."
— Madame C. J. Walker

"A creative man is motivated by the desire to achieve, not by the desire to beat others." — Ayn Rand

Courage

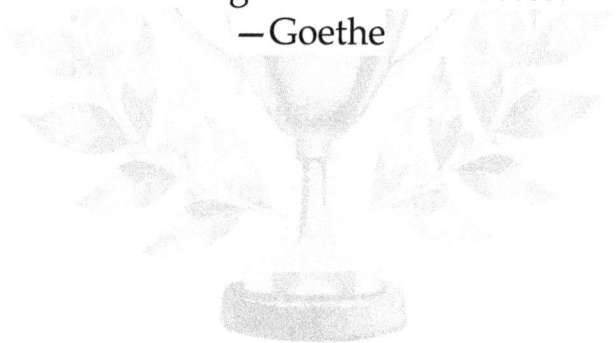

"Courage is the commitment to begin
without the guarantee of success."
—Goethe

Courage

"Courage is the most important of all the virtues, because without courage you can't practice any other virtue consistently. You can practice any virtue erratically, but nothing consistently without courage."
—Maya Angelou

"Our dreams can come true if we have the courage to pursue them."
—Walt Disney

"You cannot swim for new horizons until you have courage to lose sight of the shore."— William Faulkner

"Courage is resistance to fear, mastery of fear—not absence of fear."
— Mark Twain

"The most courageous act is still to think for yourself. Aloud." —Coco Chanel

Courage

"The great courageous act that we must all do, is to have the courage to step out of our history and past so that we can live our dreams."— Oprah Winfrey

"Courage is doing what you are afraid to do. There can be no courage unless you are scared." — Eddie Rickenbacker

"I have learned that courage is not the absence of fear, but the triumph over it. The brave man is not he who does not feel afraid, but he who conquers that fear." — Nelson Mandela

"Courage does not always roar. Sometimes courage is the silent voice at the end of the day that says, 'I will try again tomorrow'".
— Mary Anne Radmacher

Courage

"He who is not courageous enough to take risks will accomplish nothing in life." — Muhammad Ali

"Courage is not the strength to go on. It is going on when you don't have strength." — Napoleon

"Success is not final, failure is not fatal; it is the courage to continue that counts." — Winston Churchill

"You cannot be afraid to speak up and speak out for what you believe. You have to have courage, raw courage." — John Lewis

"You cannot swim for new horizons until you have courage to lose sight of the shore." — William Faulkner

Courage

"Your time is limited, so don't waste it living someone else's life. Don't be trapped by dogma which is living with the results of other people's thinking. Don't let the noise of others' opinions drown out your own inner voice. And most important, have the courage to follow your heart and intuition."
—Steve Jobs

"A man with outward courage dares to die; a man with inner courage dares to live." —Lao Tzu

"Courage is feeling fear, not getting rid of fear, and taking action in the face of fear."
— Roy T. Bennett

Discipline

"It's absolutely true that unless you can instill discipline upon yourself, you will never be able to lead others." —Zig Ziglar

Discipline

"Discipline is the bridge between goals and accomplishment." — Jim Rohn

"In vain to they talk of happiness who never subdue an impulse in obedience to a principle. He, who never sacrificed a present for a future good, or a personal to a general one, can speak of happiness only as the blind speak of color."
–Horace Mann

"Talent without discipline is like an octopus on roller skates. There's plenty of movement, but you never know if it's going to be forward, backwards or sideways." –H. Jackson Brown, Jr.

"Disciplining yourself to do what you know is right and important, although difficult, is the highroad to pride, self-esteem, and personal satisfaction."
— Margaret Thatcher

Education

"Education is the most powerful weapon
you can use to change the world."
—Nelson Mandela

Education

"Education, in the broadest of truest sense, will make an individual seek to help all people, regardless of race, regardless of color, regardless of condition." — George Washington Carver

"Education is a tree with fruit that will never cease to feed you."–Leat Kodua

"Education means emancipation. It means light and liberty. It means the uplifting of the soul of man into the glorious light of truth, the light by which men can only be made free."
— Frederick Douglass

"Real knowledge is to understand the extent of one's ignorance."–Confucius

"The only person who is educated is the one who has learned how to learn and change." — Carl Rogers

Education

"Education is that whole system of human training within and without the school house walls, which molds and develops men." — W. E. B. DuBois

"Tell me and I forget, teach me and I may remember, involve me and I learn."
— Benjamin Franklin

"Education is the passport to the future, for tomorrow belongs to those who prepare for it today." — Malcolm X

"The purpose of education...is to create in a person the ability to look at the world for himself, to make his own decisions."
— James Baldwin

"Formal education will make you a living; self-education will make you a fortune." — Jim Rohn

Education

"Develop a passion for learning. If you do, you will never cease to grow."
— Anthony J. D'Angelo

"The roots of education are bitter, but the fruit is sweet." — Aristotle

"If a man empties his purse into his head, no man can take it away from him. An investment in knowledge always pays the best interest." — Benjamin Franklin

"The difference between school and life? In school, you're taught a lesson and then given a test. In life, you're given a test that teaches you a lesson." — Tom Bodett

"He, who opens a school door, closes a prison." –Victor Hugo

Faith

"Faith is to believe what you do not see;
the reward of this faith is to see what you
believe." — Augustine of Hippo

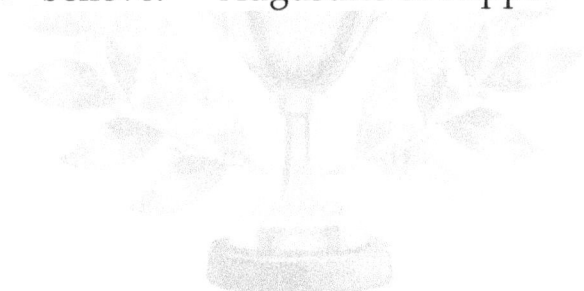

Faith

"Faith is the first factor in a life devoted to service. Without it, nothing is possible. With it, nothing is impossible."
— Mary McLeod Bethune

"He who loses money, loses much. He who loses a friend, loses much more. He who loses faith, loses all."
— Eleanor Roosevelt

"Faith is taking the first step even when you don't see the whole staircase."
–Martin Luther King, Jr.

"Faith is the strength by which a shattered world will emerge into light."
–Helen Keller

"Don't dig up in doubt what you planted in faith." -Elisabeth Elliott

"A man of courage is also full of faith."
— Marcus Tullius Cicero

Faith

"Faith is what makes life bearable, with
all its tragedies and ambiguities and
sudden, startling joys."
—Madeleine L' Engle

"Faith doesn't mean I don't question God;
faith means I've learned how to accept
the way God answers."
—Dr. Howard-John Wesley

"Faith is believing in something when
common sense tells you not to."
—Unknown

"Faith is a knowledge within the heart,
beyond the reach of proof."
– Khalil Gibran

"Without faith a man can do nothing;
with it all things are possible."
—(Sir) William Osler

Faith

"Sometimes you have to run on faith. You have to run not seeing the outcome, but just knowing that there will be the result that you desire." —Dr. D. Ivan Young

"Faith is not belief without proof, but trust without reservation."
—D. Elton Trueblood

"Faith and prayer are the vitamins of the soul; man cannot live in health without them." —Mahalia Jackson

"Faith is no irresponsible shot in the dark. It is a responsible trust in God, who knows the desires of your hearts, the dreams you are given, and the goals you have set. He will guide your paths right." —Robert Schuller

Faith

"Keep the faith, hold on. Things will get better. It might be stormy now, but it can't rain forever." — Unknown

Faith is deliberate confidence in the character of God whose ways you may not understand at the time.
– Oswald Chambers

"Faith is unseen but felt; faith is strength when we feel we have none, faith is hope when all seems lost." – Catherine Pulsifer

"When we take quantum leaps of faith, we also take quantum leaps of progress. So, trust yourself and take that leap of faith." — Unknown

Family

"The family is one of nature's masterpieces." —George Santayana

Family

"Call it a clan, call it a network, call it a tribe, call it a family: Whatever you call it, whoever you are, you need one."
—Jane Howard

"In every conceivable manner, the family is a link to our past, a bridge to our future." -Alex Haley

"No matter what you've done for yourself and for humanity if you can't look back on having given love and attention to your own family, what have you really accomplished?" —Lee Iacocca

"What can you do to promote world peace? Go home and love your family."
—Mother Teresa

"It is easier to build strong children than to repair broken men."
—Frederick Douglass

Family

"The greatest moments in life are not
concerned with selfish achievements but
rather with the things we do for the
people we love and esteem."
—Walt Disney

"The bond that links your true family is
not one of blood, but of respect and joy in
each other's life." —Richard Bach

"The child who is not embraced by the
village will burn it down to feel its
warmth." —African Proverb

"The best thing to hold onto in life is each
other." —Audrey Hepburn

"The family is the test of freedom;
because the family is the only thing that
the free man makes for himself and by
himself." —Gilbert K. Chesterton

Family

"When all the dust is settled and all the crowds are gone, the things that matter are faith, family, and friends."
— Barbara Bush

"You leave home to seek your fortune and, when you get it, you go home and share it with your family." — Anita Baker

Focus

"Whenever you want to achieve
something, keep your eyes open,
concentrate and make sure you know
exactly what you want. No one can hit
their target with their eyes closed."
— Pablo Coelho

Focus

"Identify your problems but give your power and energy to solutions."
–Tony Robbins

"The successful warrior is the average man with laser-like focus." — Bruce Lee

"Don't be distracted by criticism. Remember--the only taste of success some people get is to take a bite out of you." — Zig Ziglar

"Our greatest weapon against stress is our ability to choose one thought over another." — William James

"Focus on one thing, make it your priority, and stick with it no matter what." — Tyler Perry

Focus

"It is during our darkest moments that we must focus to see the light."
— Aristotle

"The secret of change is to focus all your energy, not on fighting the old, but building the new." — Socrates

"Your focus determines your reality."
— George Lucas

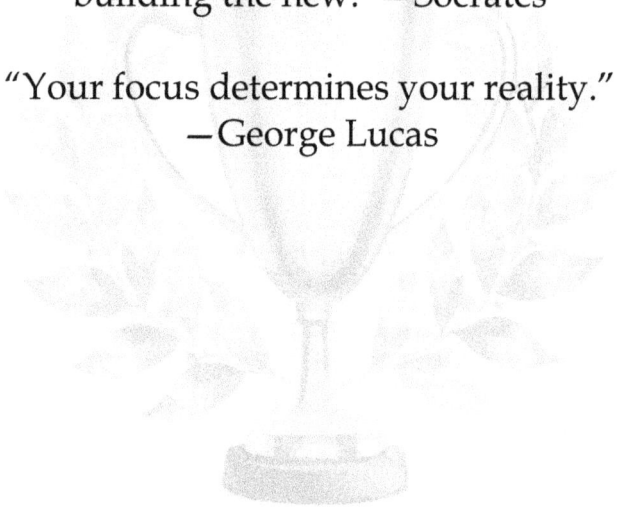

Forgiveness

"Forgiveness is about empowering yourself, rather than empowering your past." —T. D. Jakes

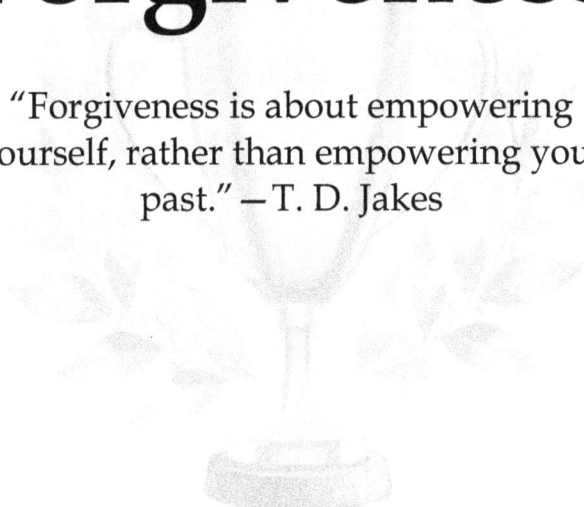

Forgiveness

"Forgiving does not erase the bitter past. A healed memory is not a deleted memory. Instead, forgiving what we cannot forget creates a new way to remember. We change the memory of our past into a hope for our future."
–Lewis B. Smedes

"The weak can never forgive. Forgiveness is the attribute of the strong."
— Mahatma Gandhi

"Resentment is like drinking poison and then hoping it will kill your enemies."
— Nelson Mandela

"When you haven't forgiven those who've hurt you, you turn your back against your future. When you do forgive, you start walking forward."
— Tyler Perry

Forgiveness

"You will know forgiveness has begun when you recall those who hurt you and feel the power to wish them well."
–Lewis B. Smedes

"He that cannot forgive others breaks the bridge over which he must pass himself; for every man has need to be forgiven."
–Thomas Fuller

"When you hold resentment toward another, you are bound to that person or condition by an emotional link that is stronger than steel. Forgiveness is the only way to dissolve that link and get free." —Catherine Ponder

"Throughout life people will make you mad, disrespect you and treat you bad. Let God deal with the things they do, cause hate in your heart will consume you too." —Will Smith

Forgiveness

"The stupid neither forgive nor forget; the naive forgive and forget; the wise forgive but do not forget."
— Thomas Szasz

"Forgiveness isn't approving what happened. It's choosing to rise above it." — Robert Sharma

"Without forgiveness life is governed by an endless cycle of resentment and retaliation." — Roberto Assagioli

"The practice of forgiveness is our most important contribution to the healing of the world."— Marianne Williamson

"True forgiveness is when you can say, 'Thank you for that experience.'"
— Oprah Winfrey

Friendship

"You can make more friends in two months by becoming interested in other people than you can in two years by trying to get other people interested in you." — Dale Carnegie

Friendship

"Don't walk behind me; I may not lead. Don't walk in front of me; I may not follow. Just walk beside me and be my friend."–Albert Camus

"The most beautiful discovery true friends make is that they can grow separately without growing apart."
— Elizabeth Foley

"An enemy is someone who increases, strengthens, encourages or enables an area of weakness in you that God wants to remove from your life."
–Dale C. Bronner

"If a man cannot keep pace with his companions, perhaps it is because he hears the beat of a different drummer. Let him step to the music he hears, however measured or far away."
— Henry David Thoreau

Friendship

"Friendship isn't about whom you have known the longest...It's about who came, and never left your side." –Unknown

"We must learn to live together as brothers or perish together as fools." –Dr. Martin Luther King, Jr.

"Keep away from people who try to belittle your ambitions. Small people always do that, but the really great make you feel that you too can become great." — Mark Twain

"As far as possible, without surrender be on good terms with all persons. Speak your truth quietly and clearly; and listen to others, even the dull and the ignorant; they too have their story."–Max Ehrmann

"I destroy my enemies when I make them friends." — Abraham Lincoln

Friendship

"People are like elevators: they can take you up and they can take you down."
–Dale C. Bronner

"The most important single ingredient in the formula of success is knowing how to get along with others."
–Theodore Roosevelt

"Associate yourself with people of good quality, for it is better to be alone than in bad company." — Booker T. Washington

"Choose people who lift you up."
— Michelle Obama

"Stay away from negative people; they a problem for every solution."
— Albert Einstein

"Surround yourself with people only who are going to take you higher."
— Oprah Winfrey

Friendship

"With reasonable men, I will reason; with humane men I will plead; but to tyrants I will give no quarter, nor waste arguments where they will certainly be lost."
— William Lloyd Garrison

"In the end, we will remember not the words of our enemies, but the silence of our friends." — Dr. Martin Luther King, Jr.

"Be who you are and say what you feel because those who mind don't matter and those who matter don't mind."
— Theodor Geisel (Dr. Seuss)

"Don't treat people as bad as they are; treat them as good as you are."
— Mother Teresa

"Everyone wants to ride with you in the limo, but what you want is someone who will take the bus with you when the limo breaks down."— Oprah Winfrey

Gratitude

"Feeling gratitude and not expressing it is like wrapping a present and not giving it." —William Arthur Ward

Gratitude

"As we express our gratitude, we must never forget that the highest appreciation is not to utter words, but to live by them"
–John F. Kennedy

"Be thankful for what you have; you'll end up having more. If you concentrate on what you don't have, you'll never, ever have enough." –Oprah Winfrey

"God gave you a gift of 86,400 seconds today. Have you used one to say, 'thank you'?" –William Arthur Ward

"When eating bamboo sprouts, remember the man who planted them."
–Chinese Proverb

"In a heart filled with gratitude, there is no room for discontentment."
— Rachel Cruze

Gratitude

"The person who hasn't ever endured difficult circumstances hasn't been born. Trouble is an integral aspect of life; there is nothing we can do to avoid it. When we nurture a grateful heart and decide to focus on what is right in our lives rather than what we perceive is wrong; we discover rich spiritual treasures buried deep beneath our tribulation. It starts with focusing on what we have instead of what we don't; and searching for the good in what we think is bad. Gratitude makes us smile despite our problems. Its transformative power helps us see light in spite of darkness. It allows us to make sense of what seems incomprehensible on the surface." –C. Chérie Hardy

"The way to develop the best that is in a person is by appreciation and encouragement." — Charles Schwab

Gratitude

"Gratitude is the healthiest of all human emotions. The more you express gratitude for what you have, the more likely you will have even more to express gratitude for." — Zig Ziglar

" 'Thank you' is the best prayer that anyone could say. I say that one a lot. Thank you expresses extreme gratitude, humility, understanding."
— Alice Walker

"I would maintain that thanks are the highest form of thought; and that gratitude is happiness doubled by wonder." — Gilbert K. Chesterton

"He is a wise man who does not grieve for the things which he has not but rejoices for those which he has."
— Epictetus

Gratitude

"Gratitude turns what we have into enough, and more. It turns denial into acceptance, chaos into order, confusion into clarity...it makes sense of our past, brings peace for today, and creates a vision for tomorrow." —Melody Beattie

"It's a funny thing about life, once you begin to take note of the things you are grateful for, you begin to lose sight of the things that you lack." —Germany Kent

"There are only two ways to live your life. One is as though nothing is a miracle. The other is as though everything is a miracle." —Albert Einstein

Hope

"Hope itself is like a star—not to be seen in the sunshine of prosperity, and only to be discovered in the night of adversity." —Charles Haddon Spurgeon

Hope

"Hope is being able to see that there is light despite all of the darkness."
— Desmond Tutu

"Hope sees the invisible, feels the intangible, and achieves the impossible." — Helen Keller

"We must accept finite disappointment, but never lose infinite hope."
— Dr. Martin Luther King, Jr.

"The best way to not feel hopeless is to get up and do something. Don't wait for good things to happen to you. If you go out and make some good things happen, you will fill the world with hope, you will fill yourself with hope." — Barack Obama

"Where there is no hope, it is incumbent on us to invent it."–Albert Camus

Hope

"Most of the important things in the world have been accomplished by people who have kept on trying when there seemed to be no hope at all."
— Dale Carnegie

"You may not always have a comfortable life and you will not always be able to solve all of the world's problems at once but don't ever underestimate the importance you can have because history has shown us that courage can be contagious and hope can take on a life of its own." — Michelle Obama

"Hope is important because it can make the present moment less difficult to bear. If we believe that tomorrow will be better, we can bear a hardship today."
— Thich Nhat Hanh

Kindness

"Love and kindness are never wasted.
They always make a difference. They
bless the one who receives them, and they
bless you, the giver."
—Barbara De Angelis

Kindness

"There are three ways to ultimate success. The first is to be kind. The second is to be kind. Third way is to be kind."
— Mr. (Fred) Rogers

"How far you go in life depend on being tender with the young; compassionate with the aged; sympathetic with the striving; and tolerant of the weak and strong because some day in life you will have been all of these."
–George Washington Carver

"Kindness is the language which the deaf can hear and the blind can see."
— Mark Twain

"Kindness in words creates confidence. Kindness in thinking creates profoundness. Kindness in giving creates love." — Lao Tzu

Kindness

"Carry out random acts of kindness, with no expectation of reward, safe in the knowledge that one day someone might do the same for you." — Princess Diana

"The only way we will survive is by being kind. The only way we can get by in this world is through the help we receive from others. No one can do it alone, no matter how great the machines are." -Amy Poehler

"No matter how busy you are, you must take time to make the other person feel important." — Mary Kay Ash

"Nearly every moment of every day, we have the opportunity to give something to someone else — our time, our love, our resources." — S. Truett Cathy

Kindness

"My daddy had taught me always to smile at people and always to make people happy to see me." — Joe Rogers, Sr.

"You never lose when you are kind; you gain so much when you demonstrate goodness to others." — C. Chérie Hardy

"When you get, give. When you learn, teach." — Maya Angelou

"Constant kindness can accomplish much. As the sun makes ice melt, kindness causes misunderstanding, mistrust, and hostility to evaporate."
— Albert Schweitzer

"A little thought and a little kindness are often worth more than a great deal of money." — John Ruskin

70

Leadership

"Leadership and learning are
indispensable to each other."
—John F. Kennedy

Leadership

"Real leaders must be ready to sacrifice all for the freedom of their people."
—Nelson Mandela

"Big pay and little responsibility are circumstances seldom found together."
–Napoleon Hill

"The secret to success is good leadership, and good leadership is all about making the lives of your team members or workers better." —Tony Dungy

"Leadership is not about titles, positions, or flowcharts. It is about one life influencing another." —John C. Maxwell

"Leaders do not avoid, repress, or deny conflict but rather see it as an opportunity." —Warren Bennis

Leadership

"It is better to lead from behind and to put others in front, especially when you celebrate victory and when nice things occur. [A leader] takes the front line when there is danger. Then people will appreciate your leadership."
–Nelson Mandela

"Enlightened leadership is spiritual if we understand spirituality not as some kind of religious dogma or ideology but as a domain of awareness where we experience values like truth, goodness, beauty, love and compassion, and also intuition, creativity, insight and focused attention." –Deepak Chopra

"If your actions inspire others to dream more, learn more, do more and become more, you are a leader."
—John Quincy Adams

Leadership

"Leadership is not being in charge, it is about taking care of people in your charge." — Simon Sinek

"If you think you're leading, but no one is following, then you are only taking a walk." — John C. Maxell

"Great leaders focus on equipping their team. It is unfair to expect what you did not equip." — Chris Hogan

"Leadership is neither a title nor a position; it is action." — Stephen R. Covey

"Leadership is the capacity to translate vision into reality." — Warren G. Bennis

"When people trust you, they will let you lead them." — C. Chérie Hardy

Learning from Failure

"If you learn from defeat, you haven't really lost." – Zig Ziglar

Learning from Failure

"The reality is that everybody makes mistakes. The issue isn't whether you will make them, it's what you will do about them. It's whether you will choose the path of humility and courage or the path of ego and pride." —Stephen R. Covey

"I never lose. I either win or learn." —Nelson Mandela

"Ninety-nine percent of the failures come from people who have the habit of making excuses." —George Washington Carver

"Defeat should not be the source of discouragement, but a stimulus to keep plotting." —Shirley Chisholm

"I have not failed. I've just found 10,000 ways that don't work." –Thomas A. Edison

Learning from Failure

"It's not the load that breaks you down, it's the way you carry it."-Lena Horne

"Don't fear failure so much that you refuse to try new things. The saddest summary of a life contains three descriptions: could have, might have and should have." –Louis E. Boone

"Failure is a bruise, not a tattoo."
–Jon Sinclair

"Failure is good. It's fertilizer."
—Rick Pitino

"Fall seven times and stand up eight."
—Japanese Proverb

"Don't fear failure; fear being successful at things that don't matter."
—Tony Dungy

Learning from Failure

"I failed my way to success."
— Thomas Edison

"Do the one thing you think you cannot do. Fail at it. Try again. Do better the second time. The only people who never tumble are those who never mount the high wire."— Oprah Winfrey

""I can accept failure. Everyone fails at something, but I cannot accept not trying." — Michael Jordan

"Failure is a stepping stone to greatness."
-Oprah Winfrey

"I've missed more than 9000 shots in my career. I've lost almost 300 games. 26 times, I've been trusted to take the game winning shot and missed. I've failed over and over and over again in my life. And that is why I succeed." — Michael Jordan

Learning from Failure

"What is success? There are many definitions, but there's one thing all the greats agree on: Success only comes by persevering despite failure."
—Jayson DeMers

"I've grown not from victories, but setbacks. If winning is God's reward, then losing is how He teaches us."
—Serena Williams

"Success is walking from failure to failure with no loss of enthusiasm."
—Winston Churchill

"If plan A fails, remember there are 25 more letters." –Chris Guillebeau

Learning from Failure

"There is only one thing that makes a dream impossible to achieve: the fear of failure." –Pablo Coelho

"The only real mistake is the one from which we learn nothing." – Henry Ford

"Failure is success if we learn from it." – Malcolm Forbes

"He who is not courageous enough to take risks will accomplish nothing in life." —Muhammad Ali

"Every adversity, every failure, every heartache carries with it the seed of an equal or greater benefit." —Napoleon Hill

"Failure is an option here. If things are not failing, you're not innovating enough." – Elon Musk

Learning from Failure

"Failure is so important. We speak about success all the time. It is the ability to resist failure or use failure that often leads to greater success. I've met people who don't want to try for fear of failing."
– J.K. Rowling

"You have to be able to accept failure to get better." – Lebron James

"Many of life's failures are people who did not realize how close they were to success when they gave up."
– Thomas Edison

"For every failure, there's an alternative course of action. You just have to find it. When you come to a roadblock, take a detour." —Mary Kay Ash

Legacy

"Carve your name on hearts, not tombstones. A legacy is etched into the minds of others and the stories they share about you." –Shannon L. Alder

Legacy

"Legacy is not leaving something for people. It's leaving something in people." — Peter Strople

"The great use of life is to spend it for something that will outlast it." — William James

"When you do something extraordinary, you create a legacy of possibilities and show others what they can do too." — Unknown

"If you would not be forgotten as soon as you are dead, either write something worth reading or do something worth writing." — Benjamin Franklin

"Be ashamed to die until you have won some victory for humanity." — Horace Mann

Legacy

"Your decisions from today forward will affect not only your life, but also your entire legacy." — Dave Ramsey

"All good men and women must take responsibility to create legacies that will take the next generation to a level we could only imagine." —Jim Rohn

"The great use of life is to spend it for something that will outlast it."
—William James

"The legacy of heroes is the memory of a great name and the inheritance of a great example." —Benjamin Disraeli

"Do not go where the path may lead, go instead where there is no path and leave a trail." —Ralph Waldo Emerson

Love

"Love will find a way through paths
where wolves fear to prey."
—George Gordon (Lord) Byron

Love

"Love recognizes no barriers. It jumps hurdles, leaps fences, and penetrates walls to arrive at its destination full of hope." — Maya Angelou

"God's love never ceases — never. Our faith does not earn it any more than our stupidity jeopardizes it. God doesn't love us less if we fail or more if we succeed. God's love never ceases." –Max Lucado

"You can love completely without complete understanding."
–Norman Maclean

"One word frees us of all the weight and pain in life. That word is love."
–Sophocles

"Love takes off masks that we fear we cannot live without and know we cannot live within." – James A. Baldwin

Love

"Be yourself. Especially do not feign affection. Neither be cynical about love, for in the face of all aridity and disenchantment, it is as perennial as the grass." —Max Ehrmann

"Darkness cannot drive out darkness, only light can do that. Hate cannot drive out hate, only love can do that."
—Dr. Martin Luther King, Jr.

"The more loving we can be, the more powerful we become."
—Silva Hartmann

"Hatred paralyzes life; love releases it. Hatred confuses life; love harmonizes it. Hatred darkens life; love illuminates it." —Dr. Martin Luther King, Jr.

Money

"Empty pockets never held anyone back. Only empty heads and empty hearts can do that." –Norman Vincent Peale

Money

"Money is an excellent servant, but a terrible master." –P. T. Barnum

"Financial peace isn't the acquisition of stuff. It's learning to live on less than you make, so you can give money back and have money to invest. You can't win until you do this." — Dave Ramsey

"For the love of money is a root of all *kinds of* evil, for which some have strayed from the faith in their greediness and pierced themselves through with many sorrows." — Paul the Apostle

"Money and success don't change people; they merely amplify what is already there." –Will Smith

"You must gain control over your money or the lack of it will forever control you."—Dave Ramsey

Money

"He that is of the opinion money will do everything may well be suspected of doing everything for money."
–Benjamin Franklin

"Rich people stay rich because they act poor and poor people stay poor because they act rich." — Lynn Richardson

"A budget is people telling their money where to go instead of wondering where it went." — Dave Ramsey

"Poverty is not an accident. Like slavery and apartheid, it is man-made and can be removed by the actions of human beings." — Nelson Mandela

"Wealth consists not in having great possessions, but in having few wants." — Epictetus

Money

"As a business owner, don't just focus on getting money but learning how to keep it. Knowledge allows us to gain, but wisdom allows us to retain what we have earned." — C. Chérie Hardy

"A wise person should have money in their head, but not in their heart."
–Jonathan Swift

"Rich people have small TVs and big libraries, and poor people have small libraries and big TVs." –Zig Ziglar

"Money is only a tool. It will take you wherever you wish, but it will not replace you as the driver." –Ayn Rand

"I have about concluded that wealth is a state of mind, and that anyone can acquire a wealthy state of mind by thinking rich thoughts." — Andrew Young

Overcoming Fear

"Each of us must confront our own fears, must come face to face with them. How we handle our fears will determine where we go with the rest of our lives. To experience adventure or to be limited by the fear of it." —Judy Blume

Overcoming Fear

"I learned that courage was not the absence of fear, but the triumph over it. The brave man is not he who does not feel afraid, but he who conquers that fear." —Nelson Mandela

"Don't let the fear of losing be greater than the excitement of winning."
—Robert Kiyosaki

"Everything you want is on the other side of fear." -Jack Canfield

"Behind me is infinite power. Before me is endless possibility. Around me is boundless opportunity. Why should I fear?" –Stella Stewart

"FEAR is an acronym for False Evidence Appearing Real." —Unknown

Overcoming Fear

"Do the thing you fear, and the death of fear is certain."' — Ralph Waldo Emerson

"Nothing in life is to be feared, it is only to be understood. Now is the time to understand more, so that we may fear less." — Marie Curie

"Fear is the main source of superstition, and one of the main sources of cruelty. To conquer fear is the beginning of wisdom." — Bertrand Russell

"One of the greatest discoveries a man makes, one of his great surprises, is to find he can do what he was afraid he couldn't do." — Henry Ford

"Fears are educated into us, and can, if we wish, be educated out." — Karl Augustus Menninger

Overcoming Fear

"Too many people are thinking of security instead of opportunity. They seem to be more afraid of life than death."
— James F. Byrnes

"Laughter is poison to fear."
— George R. R. Martin

"Fear is the enemy of hope."
—Dave Ramsey

"The greatest enemy of success is the fear of failure." —Dr. Myles Munroe

"Train yourself to let go of the things you fear to lose." —George Lucas

Patience

"Patience and perseverance have a
magical effect before which difficulties
disappear and obstacles vanish."
—John Quincy Adams

Patience

"Patience is bitter, but its fruit is sweet." — Aristotle

"One moment of patience may ward off great disaster. One moment of impatience may ruin a whole life." –Chinese Proverb

"Patience is not the ability to wait, but the ability to keep a good attitude while waiting." — Unknown

"Have patience. All things are difficult before they become easy." — Saadi Shirazi

"When you encounter various trials, big or small, be full of joy. They're opportunities to learn patience."
— Scott Curran

"Patience attracts happiness; it brings near that which is far." — Swahili Proverb

Patience

"Patience is a key element of success."
—Bill Gates

"The keys to patience are acceptance and faith. Accept things as they are and look realistically at the world around you. Have faith in yourself and in the direction you have chosen." —Ralph Marston

"He that can have patience can have what he will." —Benjamin Franklin

"Patience and fortitude conquer all things." —Ralph Waldo Emerson

"Haste makes waste." —Unknown

"Patience is one of the best security mechanisms against heartbreak."
—Dale C. Bronner

Peace

"Health does not always come from medicine. Most of the time it comes from peace of mind, peace of heart, and peace in the soul. It comes from laughter and love."—Unknown

Peace

"Peace cannot be kept by force; it can only be achieved by understanding."
–Albert Einstein

"Peace is not something you wish for. It's something you make. Something you do. Something you are. And something you give away." –Robert Fulghum

"Peace does not mean an absence of conflicts; differences will always be there. Peace means solving these differences through [constructive] means; through dialogue, education, knowledge; and through humane ways." –Dalai Lama XIV

"As far as possible, without surrender be on good terms with all persons. Speak your truth quietly and clearly; and listen to others, even the dull and the ignorant; they too have their story."
— Max Ehrmann

Peace

"Peace brings with it so many positive emotions that it is worth aiming for in all circumstances." — Estella Eliot

"If you want to make peace you don't talk to your friends. You must talk to your enemies." –Moshe Dayan

"Peace is not something you wish for. It's something you make. Something you do. Something you are. And something you give away." –Robert Fulghum

"The more tranquil a man becomes, the great is his success, his influence, his power for good. Calmness of mind is one of the beautiful jewels of wisdom." –James Allen

"Don't search for anything except peace. Try to calm the mind. Everything else will come on its own." — Baba Hari Dass

Peace

"Never be in a hurry; do everything quietly and in a calm spirit. Do not lose your inner peace for anything whatsoever, even if your whole world seems upset." — Saint Francis de Sales

"Peace can become a lens through which you see the world. Be it. Live it. Radiate it out. Peace is an inside job. — Wayne Dyer

"It isn't enough to talk about peace. One must believe in it. And it isn't enough to believe in it. One must work at it." — Eleanor Roosevelt

"Peace is a daily, a weekly, a monthly process, gradually changing opinions, slowly eroding old barriers, quietly building new structures." — John F. Kennedy

Peace

"Peace is the greatest blessing of all.
People can have health, wealth,
love, and opportunities, but if they
don't have peace within, they
cannot appreciate and enjoy
anything." — C. Chérie Hardy

"When we create peace and
harmony and balance in our minds,
we will find it in our lives."
— Louise L. Hay

"Remember that some stress is optional."
— Felicia Carmelita Hardy

"Peace comes from being able to
contribute the best that we have, and all
that we are, toward creating a world that
supports everyone."—Hafsat Abiola

Perseverance

"In the realm of ideas everything
depends on enthusiasm... in the real
world all rests on perseverance."
—Goethe

Perseverance

"You may not control all the events that happen to you, but you can decide not to be reduced by them." — Maya Angelou

"Success is not final, failure is not fatal: it is the courage to continue that counts."
–Winston Churchill

"If you really look closely, most overnight successes took a long time." — Steve Jobs

"Great works are performed not by strength but by perseverance."
— Samuel Johnson

"The key to life when it gets tough is to keep moving. Just keep moving."
— Tyler Perry

"Never give up, because you never know if the next try is going to be the one that works." — Mary Kay Ash

Perseverance

"Quitting gives those who believe in you and those who stand with you too much pain, and those who stand against you too much satisfaction."
—Dr. Dale C. Bronner

"The real test is not whether you avoid this failure, because you won't. It's whether you let it harden or shame you into inaction, or whether you learn from it; whether you choose to persevere."
—Barack Obama

"Expect trouble as an inevitable part of life and repeat to yourself, the most comforting words of all; 'this, too, shall pass.'" —Ann Landers

Power

"Power is neither good nor evil, but its user makes it so." — Erin Hunter

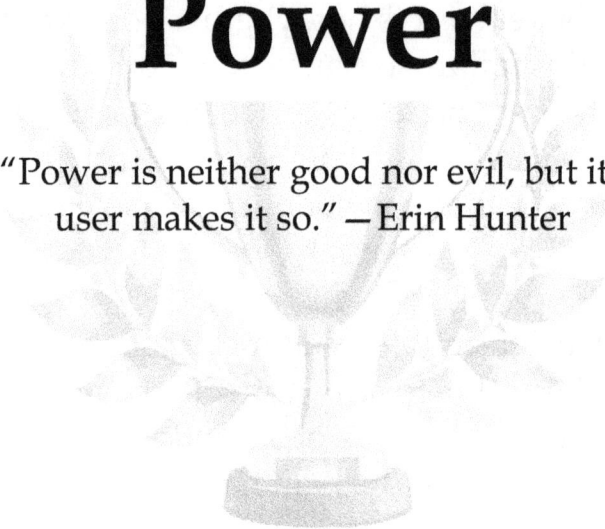

Power

"Nearly all men can stand adversity, but if you want to test a man's character, give him power." –Abraham Lincoln

"We were all born with a certain degree of power. The key to success is discovering this innate power and using it daily to deal with whatever challenges come our way." — Les Brown

"Being powerful is like being a lady. If you have to tell people you are, you aren't." — Margaret Thatcher

"Ultimately, the only power to which man should aspire is that which he exercises over himself." — Elie Wiesel

"The most common way people give up their power is by thinking they don't have any." — Alice Walker

Power

"The day the power of love overrules the love of power, the world will know peace." — Mahatma Gandhi

"The measure of a man is what he does with power." — Plato

"Power is of two kinds. One is obtained by the fear of punishment and the other by acts of love. Power based on love is a thousand times more effective and permanent then the one derived from fear of punishment." — Mahatma Gandhi

"With great power there must also come great responsibility." — Stan Lee

"Power-lust is a weed that grows only in the vacant lots of an abandoned mind." — Ayn Rand

Power

"We know that no one ever seizes power with the intention of relinquishing it."
—George Orwell

"And power without compassion is the worst kind of evil there is." —E.J. Patten

"It is said that power corrupts, but actually it's more true that power attracts the corruptible. The sane are usually attracted by other things than power."
—David Brin

"You must choose not to relinquish your power to misconceptions, fears, painful situations or people. Nothing can get in your way or prevent you from reaching your goals without your permission."
— Sheri Prentiss, M. D.

Progress

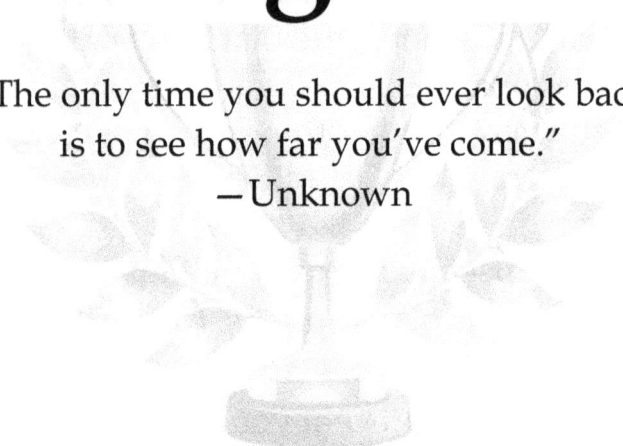

"The only time you should ever look back
is to see how far you've come."
—Unknown

Progress

"You don't make progress by standing on the sidelines, whimpering and complaining. You make progress by implementing ideas." —Shirley Chisholm

"The test of our progress is not whether we add more to the abundance of those who have much it is whether we provide enough for those who have little."
—Franklin D. Roosevelt

"The good life is a process, not a state of being. It is a direction not a destination." —Carl Rogers

"If there is no struggle, there is no progress." —Frederick Douglass

"Progress lies not in enhancing what is, but in advancing toward what will be."
—Khalil Gibran

Progress

"The man who removes a mountain begins by carrying away small stones."
–William Faulkner

"You will either step forward into growth, or you will step backward into safety." — Abraham Maslow

"What's done is done. What's gone is gone. One of life's lessons is always moving on. It's okay to look back and see how far you've come but keep moving forward." — Roy T. Bennett

"We learn more by looking for the answer to a question and not finding it than we do from learning the answer itself." — Lloyd Alexander

"All great achievements require time."
— Maya Angelou

Progress

"A journey of a thousand miles must begin with a single step." —Lao Tzu

"In the middle of a difficulty lies opportunity." —Albert Einstein

"There can be a progression to the dream; there can be steps to it. When you dissect any successful person's story, it's really rare that it was all or nothing. It's steps, and I just try to remind myself of that in terms of the things that I want; it's like, everything is a step, leading you to where you need to go." —Ava Duvernay

"Maturity: Be able to stick with a job until it is finished. Be able to bear an injustice without having to get even. Be able to carry money without spending it. Do your duty without being supervised."
—Ann Landers

Progress

"It does not matter how slowly you go as long as you do not stop." —Confucius

"Progress always involves risks. You can't steal second base and keep your foot on first." —Frederick B. Wilson

"Progress lies not in enhancing what is, but in advancing toward what will be."
—Khalil Gibran

"Under the sublime law of progress, the present outgrows the past. The great heart of humanity is heaving with the hopes of a brighter day." —Horace Mann

"Human progress never rolls in on the wheels of inevitability; it comes from the tireless efforts of men willing to be co-laborers with God."
—Dr. Martin Luther King, Jr.

Purpose

"The two most important days in your life are the day you were born and the day you find out why." —Unknown

Purpose

"Each man and woman is born into the world to do something unique and something distinctive and if he or she does not do it, it will never be done."
— Benjamin E. Mays

"He who has a why to live can bear almost any how." — Friedrich Nietzsche

"Make a difference about something other than yourselves." — Toni Morrison

"Learn to get in touch with the silence within yourself and know that everything in life has purpose. There are no mistakes, no coincidences, all events are blessings given to us to learn from."
–Elisabeth Kubler-Ross

Purpose

"We must have a theme, a goal, a purpose in our lives. If you don't know where you're aiming, you don't have a goal." — Mary Kay Ash

"Clarify your purpose. What is the why behind everything you do? When we know this in life and in design, it is empowering, and the path is clear. — Jack Canfield

"If you can't figure out your purpose, figure out your passion. For your passion will lead you right to your purpose." — T. D. Jakes

"The meaning in life is to find your gift. The purpose in life is to give it away." — Pablo Picasso

Rest

"There is virtue in work and there is virtue in rest. Use both and overlook neither." — Alan Cohen

Rest

"Slow down and enjoy life. It's not only the scenery you miss by going too fast—you also miss the sense of where you are going and why." —Eddie Cantor

"Each person deserves a day away in which no problems are confronted, no solutions searched for. Each of us needs to withdraw from the cares which will not withdraw from us." —Maya Angelou

"We will be more successful in all our endeavors if we can let go of the habit of running all the time and take little pauses to relax and re-center ourselves. And we'll also have a lot more joy in living." —Thich Nhat Hanh

"Taking time to rest ultimately allows you to do more." —C. Chérie Hardy

Service

"If you're not making someone else's life better, then you're wasting your time. Your life will become better by making other lives better."—Will Smith

Service

"Service is the rent you pay for room on this planet."-Shirley Chisholm

"Don't let what you cannot do interfere with what you can do."
—John R. Wooden

"When common people do common things in uncommon ways, they demand the attention of the world."
—George Washington Carver

"Small acts, when multiplied by millions of people, can transform the world."
—Howard Zinn

"A life of significance is about serving those who need your gifts, your leadership, your purpose." –Kevin Hall

Service

"As we lose ourselves in the service of others, we discover our own lives and our own happiness." –Dieter F. Uchtdorf

"Always render more and better service than is expected of you, no matter what your task may be." –Og Mandino

"Few of us can do great things, but all of us can do small things with great love." –Mother Teresa

"Everybody can be great because anybody can serve. You don't have to have a college degree to serve. You don't have to make your subject and verb agree to serve. You only need a heart full of grace. A soul generated by love." —Dr. Martin Luther King, Jr.

Service

"We treat our people like royalty. If you honor and serve the people who work for you, they will honor and serve you."
— Mary Kay Ash

"Success is a byproduct of being focused on serving and saving the community rather than just selling something to its members. The intrinsic reward of serving people is long lasting and incomparable to success by any other means."
— C. Chérie Hardy

"The thing that lies at the foundation of positive change, the way I see it, is service to a fellow human being." — Lee Iacocca

"When you dig another out of their troubles, you find a place to bury your own." — Unknown

Strength

"Try to look at your weakness and convert it into your strength. That's success." — Zig Ziglar

Strength

"Some people believe holding on and hanging in there are signs of great strength. However, there are times when it takes much more strength to know when to let go and then do it"
–Ann Landers

"Out of suffering have emerged the strongest souls; the most massive characters are seared with scars."
– Khalil Gibran

"Strength does not come from physical capacity. It comes from an indomitable will." –Mahatma Gandhi

"Strength does not come from winning. Your struggles develop your strengths. When you go through hardships and decide not to surrender, that is strength."– Arnold Schwarzenegger

Strength

"A hero is an ordinary individual who finds the strength to persevere and endure in spite of overwhelming obstacles."– Christopher Reeve

"Strength and growth come only through continuous effort and struggle."
—Napoleon Hill

"You never know how strong you are, until being strong is your only choice."
—Bob Marley

"All the adversity I've had in my life, all my troubles and obstacles, have strengthened me…. You may not realize it when it happens, but a kick in the teeth may be the best thing in the world for you."– Walt Disney

Strength

"Strength does not come from physical capacity. It comes from an indomitable will." — Mahatma Gandhi

"The ultimate measure of a man is not where he stands in moments of comfort and convenience, but where he stands at times of challenge and controversy."
— Dr. Martin Luther King, Jr.

"Being strong doesn't mean that you can handle every difficult situation on your own, it means that you have the sense to ask God and others for help."
— Nishan Panwar

"To live is to suffer, to survive is to find some meaning in the suffering."
— Friedrich Nietzsche

Success

"Success is not the key to happiness. Happiness is the key to success. If you love what you are doing, you will be successful." — Albert Schweitzer

Success

"Success is to be measured not so much by the position that one has reached in life as by the obstacles which he has overcome." — Booker T. Washington

"It is better to fail in originality than to succeed in imitation." — Herman Melville

"Successful people do what unsuccessful people are not willing to do. Don't wish it were easier; wish you were better." — Jim Rohn

"Success is neither magical nor mysterious. Success is the natural consequence of consistently applying basic fundamentals." — Unknown

"The only place where success comes before work is in the dictionary." — Vidal Sassoon

Success

"To achieve goals you've never achieved before, you need to start doing things you've never done before."
—Stephen R. Covey

"Success is not a random act. It arises out of a predictable and powerful set of circumstances and opportunities."
—Malcolm Gladwell

"Success is a teachable skill."
—T. Harv Eker

"The key to realizing a dream is to focus not on success but on significance -- and then even the small steps and little victories along your path will take on greater meaning."—Oprah Winfrey

"Success is liking yourself, liking what you do, and liking how you do it."
—Maya Angelou

Success

"A successful man is one who can lay a firm foundation with the bricks that others have thrown at him."
— David Brinkley

"In order to be irreplaceable, one must always be different." — Coco Chanel

"No man is ever whipped, until he quits — in his own mind."–Napoleon Hill

"The highest reward for a person's toil is not what they get for it, but what they become by it." –John Ruskin

"Genius is one percent inspiration and ninety-nine percent perspiration."
— Thomas Edison

"There is no elevator to success. You have to take the stairs." — Zig Ziglar

Success

"The price of success is hard work, dedication to the job at hand, and the determination that whether we win or lose, we have applied the best of ourselves to the task at hand."
— Vince Lombardi

"We learned about honesty and integrity - that the truth matters... that you don't take shortcuts or play by your own set of rules... and success doesn't count unless you earn it fair and square."
— Michelle Obama

"There are no secrets to success. It is the result of preparation, hard work, and learning from failure." — Colin Powell

"For true success ask yourself these four questions: Why? Why not? Why not me? Why not now?" — James Allen

Success

"The test of our [success] is not whether we add more to the abundance of those who have much; it is whether we provide enough for those who have too little."
—Franklin D. Roosevelt

"Success is no accident. It is hard work, perseverance, learning, studying, sacrifice and most of all, love of what you are doing or learning to do." —Pelé

"Don't worry about being successful but work toward being significant and the success will naturally follow."
—Oprah Winfrey

"Being successful requires being proactive and not waiting for life to come to you. It means you're on the offense, not defense. You're active, not passive."
—Benjamin P. Hardy

Success

"Your work is going to fill a large part of your life, and the only way to be truly satisfied is to do what you believe is great work. And the only way to do great work is to love what you do. If you haven't found it yet, keep looking. Don't settle. As with all matters of the heart, you'll know when you find it." —Steve Jobs

"The Lord gave us two ends - one to sit on and the other to think with. Success depends on which one we use the most." — Ann Landers

"People who succeed have momentum. The more they succeed, the more they want to succeed, and the more they find a way to succeed. Similarly, when someone is failing, the tendency is to get on a downward spiral that can even become a self-fulfilling prophecy." — Tony Robbins

Success

"The ultimate of being successful is the luxury of giving yourself the time to do what you want to do." — Leontyne Price

"Considering those who've gone before us, we shouldn't be surprised at the rough terrain and roadblocks we encounter on our journeys. While we may not understand why the Lord allows us to walk through fire and floods, it's important to remember that His intentions are to turn them into good for our lives and His glory."
— Joanna Weaver

"The definition of successful people is simply ordinary people with extraordinary determination."
— Mary Kay Ash

"Behind every successful man, there are a lot of unsuccessful years." — Unknown

Success

"The question isn't who is going to let me; it's who is going to stop me" — Ayn Rand

"I developed four rules for success in business: Be honest, work hard, equip yourself for the job, and control the growth of your company."
— Herman J. Russell

"There is no royal flower-strewn path to success. And if there is, I have not found it for I have accomplished anything in life it is because I have been willing to work hard." — Madame C. J. Walker

"The key to success is to focus on your goals, not your obstacles." — Unknown

"Achievement is talent plus preparation." — Malcolm Gladwell

Vision

"Nobody gets to live life backward. Look
ahead, that is where your future lies."
— Ann Landers

Vision

"Memory is past. It is finite. Vision is future. It is infinite. Vision is greater than history, greater than baggage, greater than the emotional scars of the past."
–Stephen R. Covey

"The real voyage of discovery consists not in seeing new landscapes but in having new eyes." –Marcel Proust

"Provision comes for people who have vision. The image you see on the inside is eventually what you'll see on the outside."–Dale C. Bronner

"If you can dream it, you can do it."
— Walt Disney

"The future belongs to those who believe in the beauty of their dreams."
— Eleanor Roosevelt

Vision

"It's not what you look at that matters, it's what you see." — Henry David Thoreau

"A great leader's courage to fulfill his vision comes from passion, not position." — John C. Maxwell

"If you don't have a vision, you're going to be stuck in what you know. And the only thing you know is what you've already seen." — Iyanla Vanzant

"If you don't design your own life plan, chances are you'll fall into someone else's plan. And guess what they have planned for you? Not much." — Jim Rohn

"In order to carry a positive action, we must develop here a positive vision."
— Dalai Lama

Vision

"Make your vision so clear that your fears become irrelevant." — Unknown

"If you want to turn a vision into reality, you have to give 100% and never stop believing in your dream."
— Arnold Schwarzenegger

"Vision without action is merely a dream. Action without vision just passes the time. Vision with action can change the world." — Joel A. Barker

"Vision without execution is hallucination." -Thomas Edison

"Create the highest grandest vision possible for your life, because you become what you believe."
— Oprah Winfrey

Vision

"Chase the vision, not the money."
— Tony Hsieh

"We are limited not by our abilities but by our vision." -Unknown

"The vision must be followed by the venture. It is not enough to stare up the steps – we must step up the stairs."
— Vance Havner

"A vision is not just a picture of what could be; it is an appeal to our better selves, a call to become something more." — Rosabeth Moss Kanter

"Don't expect people to understand your grind when God didn't give them your vision." — Unknown

Vision

"Champions aren't made in the gyms. Champions are made from something they have deep inside them — a desire, a dream, a vision." — Muhammad Ali

"When you have a vision that is strong enough and powerful enough, nothing can stand in your way." — Lewis Howes

"Where there is no vision, there is no hope." — George Washington Carver

"If you are working on something exciting that you really care about, you don't have to be pushed. The vision pulls you." — Steve Jobs

"If you create a vision for your life, doors will open." — Unknown

Vision

"A man without a vision for his future always returns to his past."
— Unknown

"Your vision will become clear only when you look into your heart. Who looks outside, dreams; who looks inside, awakens." — Unknown

"A good goal is like a strenuous exercise; it makes you stretch." — Mary Kay Ash

"It's pretty hard for the Lord to guide you if you haven't made up your mind which way to go." –Madame C. J. Walker

"It isn't a calamity to die with dreams unfulfilled, but it is a calamity not to dream." — Benjamin E. Mays

Wisdom

"In the moment of crisis, the wise build
bridges and the foolish build dams."
— Nigerian Proverb

Wisdom

"By three methods we may learn wisdom: First, by reflection, which is the noblest; second, by imitation, which is easiest; and third by experience, which is the bitterest." –Confucius

"From the errors of others, a wise man corrects his own."–Publilius Syrus

"The fool wonders, the wise man asks." — Benjamin Disraeli

"The doorstep to the temple of wisdom is a knowledge of our own ignorance." — Benjamin Franklin

"Turn your wounds into wisdom." — Oprah Winfrey

"Wisdom outweighs any wealth." —Sophocles

Wisdom

"Wisdom is not a product of schooling but of the lifelong attempt to acquire it." — Albert Einstein

"Knowledge speaks, but wisdom listens." — Jimi Hendrix

"A fool is known by his speech; and a wise man by silence." — Pythagoras

"One part of wisdom is knowing what you don't need anymore, and letting it go." — Jane Fonda

"We don't receive wisdom; we must discover it for ourselves after a journey that no one can take for us or spare us." — Marcel Proust

Wisdom

"Real wisdom is not the knowledge of everything, but the knowledge of which things in life are necessary, which are less necessary, and which are completely unnecessary to know."
— Leo Tolstoy

"Earthly wisdom is doing what comes naturally. Godly wisdom is doing what the Holy Spirit compels us to do."
— Charles Stanley

"Without wisdom, the future has no meaning, no valuable purpose."
— Herbie Hancock

"Wisdom is the right use of knowledge. To know is not to be wise. Many men know a great deal… There is no fool so great a fool as a knowing fool. But to know how to use knowledge is to have wisdom." — Charles Spurgeon

Bibliography

Abiola, Hafsat (1945) Nigerian human rights activist

Adams, John Quincy (1767-1843) Former US president and statesman

Alder, Shannon

Ali, Muhammad (1942-2016) American boxer, activist and philanthropist

Alexander, Lloyd (1805–1872) American politician

Angelou, Maya (1928–2014) American writer and civil rights activist

Aristotle (384-322 BC) Greek philosopher and mathematician

Ash, Mary Kay (1918-2001) American businesswoman and author

Assagioli, Roberto (1888–1974) Italian psychiatrist and pioneer

Augustine of Hippo (354-430 AD) Roman-African theologian, philosopher, writer, and saint

Bach, Richard (1936) American writer

Bibliography

Baker, Anita (1958) American singer and songwriter

Baldwin, James (1924-1987) American writer and activist

Barker, Joel A. (?) American lecturer and author

Barnum, P. T. (1810–1891) American businessman and politician

Beattie, Melody (1948) American author

Bennett, Roy T. (1939-2014) American politician

Bethune, Mary McLeod (1875-1955) American educator, humanitarian and civil right activist

Blume, Judy (1938) American writer

Bodett, Tom (1955) American author, radio host and voice actor

Bojaxhiu, Mary Teresa "Mother Teresa" (1910-1997) Albanian-Indian nun, missionary, and Nobel Prize laureate

Bonaparte, Napoleon (1769-1821) French emperor and military leader

Bibliography

Boone, Louis E. (1941–2005) American writer

Breedlove, Sarah aka "Madame C. J. Walker" (1867-1919) American businesswoman, social and political activist, and philanthropist

Brin, David (1950) American scientist and author

Brinkley, David (1920-2003) American broadcast journalist

Bronner, Dale C. (1962) American minster and author

Brown Jr., H. Jackson (1940) American inspirational author

Brown, Les (1945) American motivational speaker and author

Buffet, Warren (1930) American businessman and philanthropist

Bush, Barbara (1925-2018) American former first lady and humanitarian

Byrnes, James F. (1882-1972) American judge and politician

151

Bibliography

Byron, George Gordon (1788-1824)
English poet and politician
Camus, Albert (1913-1960) French-
Algerian writer, philosopher and Nobel
Prize laureate
Canfield, Jack (1944) American author
and motivational speaker
Cantor, Eddie (1892-1964) American
entertainer
Carnegie, Dale (1888-1955) American
author and lecturer
Carver, George Washington (1864-1943)
American scientist and inventor
Cathy, S. Truett (1921-2014) American
businessman, investor, author, and
philanthropist
Chambers, Oswald (1874-1917) Scottish
teacher and minister
Chanel, Coco (1883-1971) French fashion
designer and businesswoman
Chesterton, Gilbert K. (1874-1936)
English writer and philosopher

Bibliography

Chisholm, Shirley (1924-2005) American politician, educator, and author

Chopra, Deepak (1946) Indian-American author and doctor

Churchill, Winston (1874-1965) British politician, military leader and author

Cicero, Marcus Tullius (106-43 BC) Roman philosopher, statesman, author, lawyer, and orator

Coelho, Pablo (1947) Brazilian writer

Cohen, Alan (1950) American writer

Confucius (551-479 BC) Chinese philosopher and politician

Covey, Stephen R. (1932-2012) American author and businessman

Cruze, Rachel (1988) American author

Curie, Marie (1867-1934) Polish-French scientist, Nobel Prize laureate

Curran, Scott (1957) Canadian writer

De Angelis, Barbara (1951) American author and psychologist

D'Angelo, Anthony J. (?) American writer

153

Bibliography

Dass, Baba Hari (1923-2018) Indian yoga master and monk

Dayan, Moshe (1915-1981) Israeli military leader and politician

DeMers, Jayson (?) American writer and entrepreneur

Disney, Walt (1901-1966) American businessman, animator, and film producer

Disraeli, Benjamin (1804-1881) British politician

Douglass, Frederick (1818-1895) American abolitionist, writer, and orator

Du Bois, W. E. B. (1868-1963) American historian, writer and civil rights activist

Dungy, Tony (1955) former NFL player and coach, writer and mentor

Durant, Will (1885-1981) American historian and writer

Duvernay, Ava (1972) American film director

Dyer, Wayne (1940-2015) American author and motivational speaker

154

Bibliography

Edison, Thomas (1847-1931) American inventor and businessman

Ehrmann, Max (1872-1945) American writer and attorney

Einstein, Albert (1879-1955) German-American physicist and philosopher

Eker, T. Harv (1954) Canadian author, businessman, and motivational speaker

Eliot, Estella (?) American poet

Elliot, Elisabeth (1926-2015) American author and inspirational speaker

Emerson, Ralph Waldo (1803-1882) American lecturer, philosopher and writer

Epictetus (50-135 AD) Greek philosopher

Fargo, Tim (?) American author and entrepreneur

Faulkner, William (1897-1962) American writer and Nobel Prize laureate

Foley, Elizabeth (1965) American author, professor, and lawyer

Fonda, Jane (1937) American actress and political activist

Bibliography

Forbes, Malcolm (1919-1990) American entrepreneur and publisher
Ford, Henry (1863-1947) American business magnate
Franklin, Benjamin (1706-1790) American statesman, scientist, writer, politician, philosopher, and inventor
Fulghum, Robert (1937) American writer and minister
Fuller, Thomas (1608-1661) English writer, historian and minister
Garrison, William Lloyd (1805-1879) American journalist and civil rights activist
Gandhi, Mahatma (1869-1948) Indian lawyer and civil rights activist
Gates, Bill (1955) American business magnate, software developer, and philanthropist
Geisel, Theodor (1904-1991) American writer, illustrator, cartoonist, screenwriter, and filmmaker

156

Bibliography

Gibran, Khalil (1883-1931) Lebanese-American writer, artist and philosopher

Gladwell, Malcolm (1963) Canadian author, journalist and lecturer

Goethe, Johann Wolfgang von (1749-1832) German writer and statesman

Guillebeau, Chris (1978) American author and blogger

Haley, Alex (1921-1992) American author and journalist

Hall, Kevin (1955-1991) American actor

Hancock, Herbie (1940) American musician, composer, and actor

Hanh, Thich Nhat (1926) Vietnamese Buddhist monk and peace activist

Hardy, Benjamin P. (?) American author and psychologist

Hardy, C. Chérie (1965) American educator and author

Hardy, Felicia C. (1990) American author

Hartmann, Silvia (?) American author

Havner, Vance (1901 -1986) American minister and author

Bibliography

Hay, Louise L. (1926-2017) American author and motivational speaker

Height, Dorothy (1912-2010) American civil rights activist

Hendrix, Jimi (1942-1970) American musician and songwriter

Hepburn, Audrey (1929-1993) British actress and humanitarian

Hill, Napoleon (1883-1970) American author

Hilton, Sr., Conrad N. (1887-1979) American hotelier and philanthropist

Hogan, Chris (1988) American football player (NFL)

Horne, Lena (1917-2019) American entertainer and civil rights activist

Howard, Jane Elizabeth (1923-2014) English novelist

Howes, Lewis (1983) American author, and former professional athlete

Hsieh, Tony (1973) Taiwanese-American entrepreneur

Bibliography

Hugo, Victor (1802-1885) French novelist, poet, and artist

Hunter, Erin (?) American penname for several fantasy novelists

Iacocca, Lee (1924-2019) American businessman, author and philanthropist

Jackson, Mahalia (1911-1972) American gospel singer and civil rights activist

Kanter, Rosabeth Moss (1943) American Professor

Keller, Helen (1880-1968) American author, political activist, and lecturer

Kennedy, John F. (1917-1963) Former US president, military hero and author

Kent, Germany (?) American author, professor and historian

King, Coretta Scott (1927-2006) American civil rights leader and author

King, Jr., Martin Luther (1929-1968) American civil rights leader, minister, author, and Nobel Prize laureate

Bibliography

Kiyosaki, Robert (1947) American businessman and author

Kodua, Leat (?) Ghanaian-American educator

Kubler-Ross, Elisabeth (1926-2004) Swiss-American psychiatrist and author

Jakes, T. D. (1957) American minister, author and filmmaker

James, Lebron (1984) American basketball player (NBA) and philanthropist

James, William (1842-1910) American psychologist, professor and author

Jobs, Steve (1955-2011) American business magnate and engineer

Jordan, Michael (1963) Former basketball player (NBA), businessman and philanthropist

Landers, Ann (1918-2002) American columnist

Lauder, Estée (1906-2004) American businesswoman

Bibliography

Lee, Bruce (1940-1973) Chinese-American martial arts expert and instructor, actor, film director, and philosopher

Lee, Stan (1922-2018) American comic book writer and illustrator, editor, publisher, and film producer

L'Engle, Madeleine (1918-2007) American author

Lewis, John (1940) American civil rights leader, politician, and author

Lincoln, Abraham (1809-1865) Former US president, statesman, and lawyer

Lombardi, Vincent Thomas (1913-1970) American football player, coach, and executive (NFL)

Lucado, Max (1955) American minister and author

Lucas, George (1944) American filmmaker, screenwriter, producer, businessman, and philanthropist

Maclean, Norman (1902-1990) American author, and professor

Bibliography

Mandela, Nelson (1918-2013) South African civil rights activist, lawyer, political leader, author, philanthropist, and Nobel Prize laureate

Mandino, Augustine "Og" (1923-1996) American author and motivational speaker

Mann, Horace (1759-1859) American educational reformer and politician

Marley, Robert Nesta "Bob" (1945-1981) Jamaican singer, songwriter, and musician

Marston, Ralph (1907-1967) American football player (NFL) and motivational speaker

Martin, George R. R. (1948) American novelist, screenwriter, and television producer

Maslow, Abraham (1908-1970) American psychologist and writer

Maxwell, John C. (1947) American author, minister, and motivational speaker

Bibliography

Mays, Benjamin E. (1894-1984) American minister, educational leader, and civil rights leader

Mead, Margaret (1901-1978) American cultural anthropologist, author and motivational speaker

Melville, Herman (1819-1891) American writer

Menninger, Karl Augustus (1893-1990) American psychiatrist and writer

Miles, James (1829-1871) American military hero

Morrison, Toni (1931-2019) American writer, professor and Nobel Prize laureate

Munroe, Myles (1954-2014) Bahamian minister and author

Musk, Elon (1971) South African-American engineer, technological magnate, and entrepreneur

Nascimento, Edson Arantes do "Pelé" (1940) Brazilian professional soccer player and sports ambassador

Bibliography

Nietzsche, Friedrich (1844-1900) German philosopher, writer, and cultural critic

Obama, Barack Hussein (1963) former US president, politician, author, philanthropist, and Nobel Prize laureate

Obama, Michelle (1964) American lawyer, author, and former US first lady

Orwell, George (1903-1950) English writer

Osler, William (1849-1919) Canadian physician and professor

Panwar, Nishan (1989) Indian writer

Patten, E. J. (1974) American author

Paul, the Apostle (?-c. 62-64 AD) Turkish religious leader

Peale, Norman Vincent (1898-1993) American minister, author, and motivational speaker

Perry, Tyler (1969) American filmmaker, director and producer, screenwriter, actor, author, and philanthropist

Bibliography

Picasso, Pablo (1881-1973) Spanish painter, sculptor, printmaker, ceramicist, stage designer, poet, and playwright

Pitino, Rick (1952) American professional basketball coach

Plato (c. 428 BC – c. 348 BC) Greek philosopher and writer

Poehler, Amy (1971) American actress, comedian, writer, producer, and director.

Ponder, Catherine (1927) American minister and author

Powell, Colin (1937) American (retired) army general, politician, and author

Prentiss, Sheri (?) American physician, author, and breast cancer survivor

Price, Leontyne (1927) American singer

Princess Diana (1961-1997) British princess, educator, and philanthropist

Proust, Marcel (1871-1922) French writer and philosopher

Pulsifer, Catherine (?) American writer

Bibliography

Pythagoras (c. 570 – c. 795 BC) Greek philosopher and teacher

Radmacher, Mary Anne (?) American writer, artist, trainer, and speaker

Ramsey III, David Lawrence "Dave" (1960) American financial advisor, radio show host, businessman, and author

Rand, Ayn (1905-1982) Russian-American writer and philosopher

Reeve, Christopher (1952-2004) American actor, film director and writer

Richardson, Lynn (?) American author

Rickenbacker, Eddie (1890-1973) American military hero, race car driver, and automotive designer

Robbins, Tony (1960) American motivational speaker, author, and philanthropist

Robinson, Jackie (1919-1972) American baseball player (MLB and NL), civil rights activist

Bibliography

Rogers, Carl (1902-1987) American psychologist, professor, and author

Rogers, Fred (1928-2003) American television pioneer, producer, puppeteer, writer, musician, and minister

Rogers Sr., Joe (1919-2017) American business man and philanthropist

Rohn, Jim (1930-2009) American business and motivational speaker

Roosevelt, Eleanor (1884-1962) American human rights activist and former US first lady

Roosevelt, Franklin D. (1882-1945) former US president, lawyer, and politician

Roosevelt, Theodore (1858-1919) Former US president, statesman, politician, conservationist, naturalist, and writer

Rowling, J. K. (1965) British author, film producer, television producer, screenwriter, and philanthropist

Bibliography

Ruskin, John (1819-1900) English artist, philosopher, and philanthropist

Russell, Bertrand (1872-1970) British philosopher, logician, mathematician, historian, writer, essayist, social critic, political activist, and Nobel Prize laureate

Russell, Herman J. (1930-2014) American entrepreneur, community leader, author, and philanthropist

Sadat, Anwar (1918-1981) Former Egyptian president and Nobel Prize laureate

Sales, Francis de (1567-1622) French theologian, writer, and saint

Santayana, George (1863-1952) Spanish novelist, poet, professor, and philosopher

Schuller, Robert (1926-2015) American minister, author, and motivational speaker

Schwab, Charles (1937) American investor, financial executive, and philanthropist

Bibliography

Schwarzenegger, Arnold (1947)
Austrian-American actor, filmmaker,
businessman, author, politician, and
former professional bodybuilder
Schweitzer, Albert (1875-1965) French-
German theologian, philosopher, writer,
physician, humanitarian, musician and
Nobel Prize laureate
Sharma, Robin (1964) Canadian writer
and lawyer
Shirazi, Saadi (1210-1291) Persian writer
Sinclair, John (1941) American political
activist, poet, and writer
Sinek, Simon (1973) British-American
author and motivational speaker
Smith, Will (1968) American actor, film
producer, musician, and philanthropist
Socrates (469-399 BC) Greek educator,
philosopher, and orator
Sophocles (c. 497- c. 406 BC) Greek
playwright and philosopher

Bibliography

Smedes, Lewis B. (1921-2002) American theologian and author

Spurgeon, Charles Haddon (1934-1892) English minister, abolitionist, and author

Stanley, Charles (1932) American minister and author

Stewart, Stella (?) American author

Strople, Peter (?) American author and businessman

Swift, Jonathan (1667-1745) Anglo-Irish author

Swindoll, Charles (1934) American minister, author, educator, and radio host

Syrus, Publilius (85 – 43 BC) – Syrian-Roman writer

Szasz, Thomas (1920-2012) Hungarian-American psychiatrist, psychoanalyst, professor, and author

Thatcher, Margaret (1925-2013) Former British prime minister, stateswoman and author

Bibliography

Thoreau, Henry David (1817-1862) American essayist, poet, journalist, and philosopher

Tolstoy, Leo (1828-1910) Russian novelist, philosopher, and religious leader

Trueblood, D. Elton (1900-1994) American theologian, chaplain, and author

Tutu, Desmond (1931) South African theologian, human rights activist, and Nobel Prize laureate

Twain, Mark (1835-1910) American writer, humorist, and lecturer

Tzu, Lao (?) Chinese Philosopher and teacher

Uchtdorf, Dieter F. (1940) German aviator, airline executive, religious leader and author

Vanzant, Iyanla (1953) American life coach, author, television personality, spiritual teacher, and lawyer

Walker, Alice (1944) American writer

Bibliography

Ward, William A. (1921-1994) American inspirational writer

Washington, Booker T. (1856-1915) American educational leader, author, orator, and US presidential advisor

Weaver, Joanna (?) American writer

Wesley, Howard-John (1976) American minister

Wheatley, Margaret "Meg" (1944) American leadership consultant, researcher, professor, and author

Wiesel, Elie (1928-2016) Romanian-American writer, teacher, human rights activist, and Nobel Prize laureate

Wilcox, Frederick B. (?) American author

Williams, Serena (1981) American tennis champion, businesswoman, and philanthropist

Williamson, Marianne (1952) American author, spiritual leader, politician, and activist.

172

Bibliography

Winfrey, Oprah (1954) American media magnate, television personality, film producer, author, actress, human rights activist, and philanthropist

Wooden, John C. (1910-2010) American basketball player (college) and coach

Young, D. Ivan (?) American life coach, professor, and radio host

X, Malcolm (né Malcolm Little) (1925-1965) American minister and civil rights activist

Young, Andrew (1932) American civil rights leader, politician, ambassador, minister, author, and philanthropist

Ziglar, Zig (1926-2012) American author, salesman, and motivational speaker

Zinn, Howard (1922-2010) American historian, professor, writer, and civil rights activist

Every effort was made to give accurate credit for each quote. Please contact us at avantgardebooks@gmail.com if you see something that needs to be changed. Thank you in advance for your support.